BUNNIES

"He who fears ~~being conquered~~ is sure of defeat."

— Napoleon Bonaparte

For Mom, Dad & Erika — where my history began — J.F.F.

For my nephews — A.K.

ACKNOWLEDGMENTS

Special thanks to Dr. Kelly Summers, Assistant Professor of History at MacEwan University, Alberta, and Dr. Christopher Tozzi, Senior Lecturer in Humanities and Social Sciences at Rensselaer Polytechnic Institute, New York, for reading the manuscript and offering valuable notes on historical accuracy.

Published in Canada and the U.S. by Kids Can Press Ltd.
25 Dockside Drive, Toronto, ON M5A 0B5

Kids Can Press is a Corus Entertainment Inc. company

www.kidscanpress.com

The artwork in this book was drawn in ink and colored digitally in Photoshop.
The text is set in Supernett.

Edited by Yasemin Uçar
Designed by Andrew Dupuis

Printed and bound in Dongguan, Guangdong, P.R. China, in 10/2020 by Toppan Leefung

CM 21 0 9 8 7 6 5 4 3 2 1

LIBRARY AND ARCHIVES CANADA CATALOGUING IN PUBLICATION

Title: Napoleon vs. the bunnies / written by Jenny Fox ; illustrated by Anna Kwan.
Other titles: Napoleon versus the bunnies
Names: Fox, Jennifer, 1976– author. | Kwan, Anna, 1991– illustrator.
Description: Series statement: Head-to-head history
Identifiers: Canadiana 20200236741 | ISBN 9781525302022 (hardcover)
Classification: LCC PZ7.1.F69 Nap 2021 | DDC j813/.6 — dc23

Kids Can Press gratefully acknowledges that the land on which our office is located is the traditional territory of many nations, including the Mississaugas of the Credit, the Anishnabeg, the Chippewa, the Haudenosaunee and the Wendat peoples, and is now home to many diverse First Nations, Inuit and Métis peoples.

We thank the Government of Ontario, through Ontario Creates; the Ontario Arts Council; the Canada Council for the Arts; and the Government of Canada for supporting our publishing activity.

HEAD-TO-HEAD HISTORY

NAPOLEON VS. THE BUNNIES

J. F. Fox

Anna Kwan

Kids Can Press

This is Napoleon, one of the greatest generals in history.
He was not a big man, but he did big things.

He commanded the French Army, one of the most powerful in the world. He fought bravely alongside his men, conquering lands across Europe and beyond.

He became emperor of France and put in place new laws.

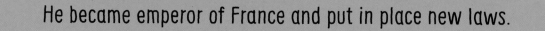

Crowds cheered for him. Soldiers adored him.

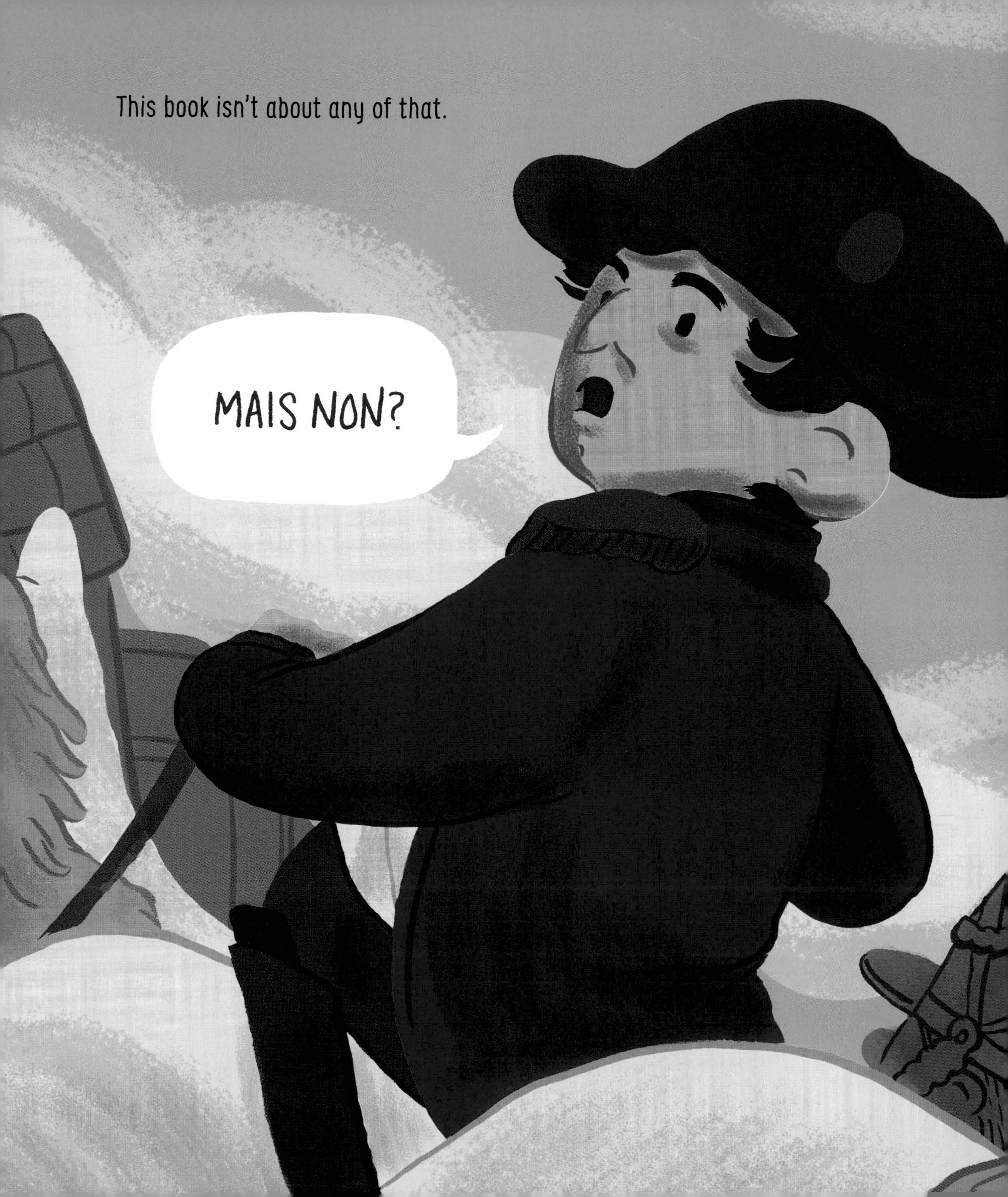
This book isn't about any of that.
MAIS NON?

Non. This book is about the time the great Napoleon battled with bunnies.

LES FLUFFY BUNNEEZ?

That's right, fluffy little bunnies.

Let's go back to the summer of 1807.

Napoleon and Tsar Alexander of Russia agreed to stop fighting. To seal their promise, they signed a treaty. They did it in neutral territory — on a raft, in the middle of a river.

The war with Russia was over. It was time for Napoleon to have some fun. He ordered his chief of staff, Louis-Alexandre (let's call him "Louie" for short), to organize a festive day with a rabbit hunt.

Louie searched the countryside for every bunny he could find.
He rounded up hundreds of rabbits.
Maybe even thousands.

BEAUCOUP DE LAPINS!

Did we mention how cute they were?

On the day of the hunt, the fearless general stood ready.
A horn blew. Cages opened. Bunnies burst forth!

There was just one little problem.

The bunnies didn't hippity-hop for their lives.

Quite the opposite! They made a beeline straight for Napoleon.

You see, the rabbits Louie had collected were not wild.

They had grown up on farms — farms where they were fed by people.

The great Napoleon was surrounded.
The army of rabbits advanced. Napoleon and
his men jumped, swung and swatted.

It was no use.

The bunny battalion zeroed in.

When they were just inches away, the bunnies unleashed the most devastating weapon in their entire arsenal — the game changer, the *coup de grâce* ...

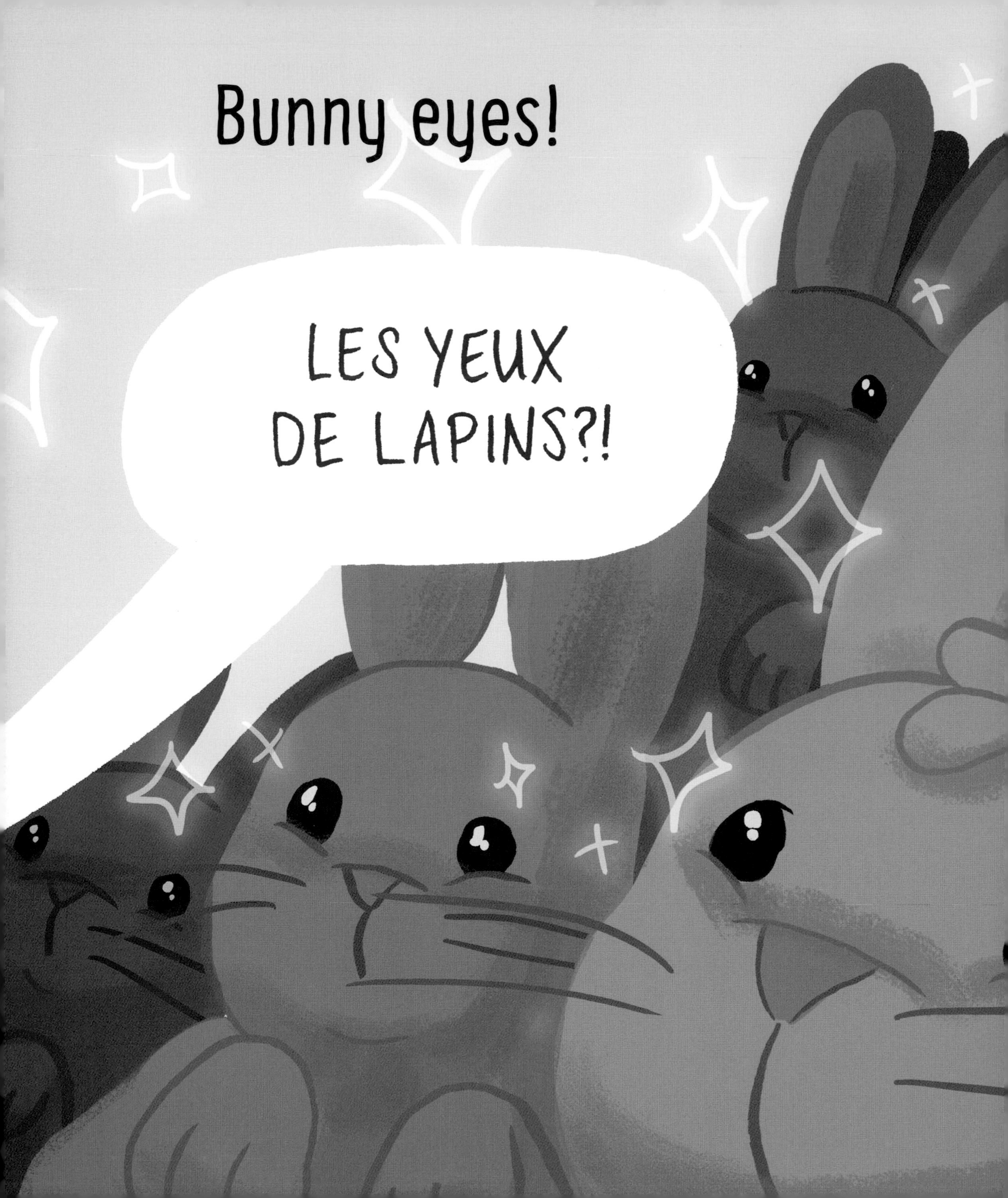
Bunny eyes!
LES YEUX DE LAPINS?!

Now, Napoleon was a pretty tough customer.

He'd marched thousands of miles,

camped with his men in the harshest conditions

and ridden into cannon fire without a second thought.

Still, everyone — even the bravest of the brave — is scared of something. And when those bunnies reached the edge of his fancy little hunting coat, the great general, His Imperial and Royal Majesty, Emperor of the French, King of Italy ...

PROTECTOR OF THE CONFEDERATION OF THE RHINE ...

... turned and fled!

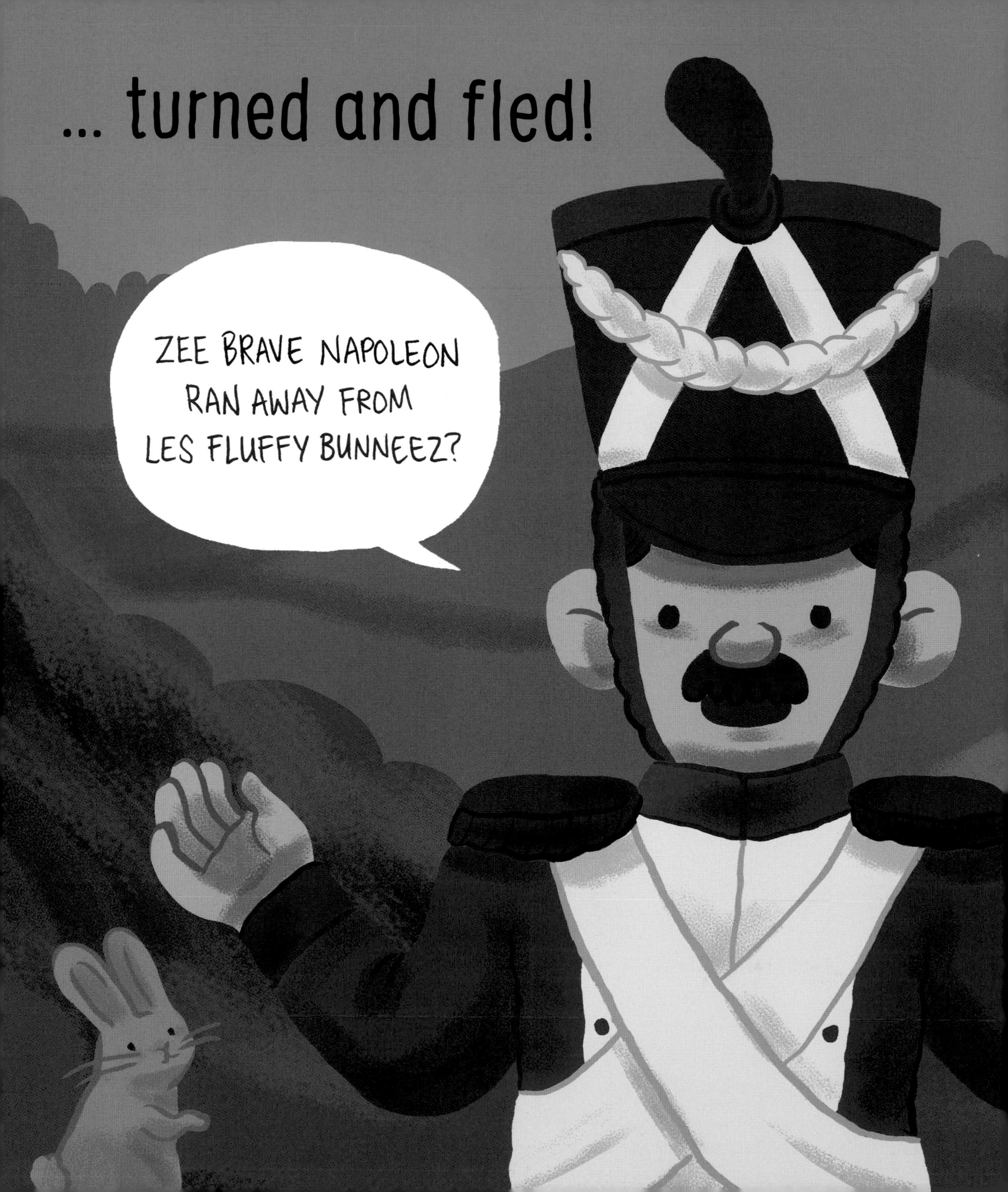

Oui. The brave Napoleon hightailed it out of there like his breeches were on fire.

Why was Napoleon so unnerved by a bunch of bunnies? We may never know.

After the ill-fated hunt, he would go on to win many more battles and lose a few, too. His reign ended at the epic Battle of Waterloo.

But try telling that to the rabbits.

NAPOLEON vs. HISTORY

Napoleon fought sixty major battles and lost only seven — eight if you count the fateful day with the bunnies. As a military leader, he ranks with legends such as Alexander the Great, Julius Caesar, Genghis Khan and George Washington — but how should history judge him? Was he good or bad? A success or failure? It's not a simple answer. See what you think.

STRENGTHS

- *Bravery* — Napoleon was fearless in the face of battles.
- *Calm* — Even as bullets flew, he coolly made decisions.
- *Humor* — Napoleon joked around with his soldiers.
- *Smarts* — A huge reader, he loved history and math.

WEAKNESSES

- *Arrogance* — Napoleon felt it was his right to rule others.
- *Brutality* — He crushed rebellions and burned villages.
- *Greed* — He always wanted more: wealth, power, glory.
- *Insecurity* — Napoleon hated criticism and looking weak.

HISTORIC HIGHLIGHTS

- Napoleon called the **Napoleonic Code** his "glory." This clearer new system of laws limited how much power the Church, kings and nobles had over everyday life. It granted citizens — including peasants — religious freedom and rights to self-expression, and awarded jobs based on skill instead of nobility. (Not all of the laws were fair, though. Slavery was permitted in French colonies and men had more rights than women.)

- In 1815, Napoleon pulled off one of history's great escapes! While briefly exiled to the island of Elba near Italy, he sneaked aboard a ship and fled back to France. He quickly raised a new army and regained control of the country.

FAMOUS FAILS

- The clever strategist made a mega mistake **invading Russia in 1812**. Roads were rough and winter was brutal. Supplies couldn't reach Napoleon's army. Between the battles and the lack of food and warm clothing, as many as 500 000 French soldiers died.

- At the **Battle of Waterloo**, in 1815 in modern-day Belgium, the British and their allies defeated the French army. It was Napoleon's last stand. To keep him from escaping exile again, he was sent to St. Helena, a faraway island between Africa and South America.

However *you* judge Napoleon's story, we know it ended on May 5, 1821. The once-powerful general died of cancer at the age of fifty-one on that "cursed rock," St. Helena, far from his beloved France … and all of its scary bunnies.

GLOSSARY

arsenal: a collection, or supply, of weapons, often belonging to an army

battalion: a large force of soldiers or troops, usually organized into smaller groups

Battle of Waterloo: Napoleon's final battle, where he lost power forever; a "Waterloo" or "Waterloo moment" has come to mean an ultimate challenge

breeches: short, typically knee-length, pants worn from the 1500s to 1800s

coup de grâce: a final strike or death blow, translated as "stroke, or blow, of mercy"

emperor: a ruler of a large territory, sometimes made up of more than one country

exile: a punishment of being sent away from one's own country

general: the highest ranking military officer, who commands entire armies and plans their movements in battles

Napoleonic Code: also called the French Civil Code, a system of laws that came into effect in 1804 under Napoleon's leadership. Before the Code, France did not have a single set of laws that were applied in a consistent way across the country. The Code strongly influenced laws across Europe and in French colonies.

neutral (territory): not part of one country or another; not supporting or favoring either side

nobility (or noble class): a group of people born with titles, land and/or wealth

peasant: a person of low social status, usually a farmer, who worked for others and did not have wealth

rebellion: an uprising against the leader or government in charge

treaty: a signed agreement between two countries, often to end a war

tsar (or czar): a monarch or ruler, typically in Russia

SOURCES

Bone, Matthew, and Bruce Burgess, producers. *Private Lives of the Monarchs*. Season 2, episode 1: "Napoleon Bonaparte." Aired May 18, 2020, on Smithsonian Channel. London, UK: Like a Shot Entertainment.

Chandler, David G. *The Campaigns of Napoleon*. London: Weidenfeld & Nicolson, 1995.

Raj, Rishi. "Innocent Long-Eared Bunnies: A Nightmare for Napoleon." Medium, November 5, 2018. Retrieved from https://medium.com/@theindianrishi/innocent-long-eared-bunnies-a-nightmare-for-napoleon-a739a0c7748c.

Reilly, Lucas. "The Time Napoleon Was Attacked by Rabbits." Mental Floss, June 26, 2013. Retrieved from https://www.mentalfloss.com/article/51364/time-napoleon-was-attacked-rabbits.

Roberts, Andrew. *Napoleon: A Life*. New York: Penguin Books, 2015.

Zamoyski, Adam. *Napoleon: A Life*. New York: Hachette Book Group, 2018.